Japanese For Beginners:

Grow Your Vocabulary & Increase Your Conversational Fluency

Takumi Nonaka

i

Table of contents

Introduction

Scripts

In Japanese, Japan is called 'Nihon' or 'Nippon,' and counter 'go' means 'language' in Japanese. Thus, the Japanese language is named 'Nihongo' in Japan. There are three types of scripts in the Japanese language, namely Hiragana, Katakana, and Kanji. Hiragana is used for basic Japanese in Japan. Let me introduce you to these three scripts.

Kanji

Let us travel the world today from Greece to Japan at the beginning of this book. We will notice that if we follow the Silk Road (an ancient path which was used for trading of silk and then became very crucial in terms of cultural, political, economic, and religious exchange. It connects many countries from Greece to China for trading purposes) from Greece to China, later on, Korea followed China and Japan followed Korea. Thus if someone from among you is aware of Korean dramas or has tried watching them with subtitles or even if you know a little about the Japanese language, you will understand that a few of the Chinese characters, Korean characters, and Japanese characters resemble each other. Around 2000 years ago, Chinese script entered Japan through official seals on mirrors, letters, and all decorative objects imported from China. Before this, Japan didn't have a written language. As some time passed, due to certain requirements, Japanese literature accepted these characters. And this is how Kanji came to Japan.

A few specifications of Kanji:

• The word 'Kanji' has evolved from 'Han characters' in China.

• Kanji is a pictorial representation of an object.

• The complicated kanjis are the combination of two or more basic radicals. There are a total of 214 radicals.

• Every Kanji has some meaning. A few of the examples are mentioned below.

See, in childhood, we all used to make a drawing in our drawing class. We used to present nature with a small house, a huge tree, mountains, sun, birds, and the river. The way we used to represent the river is exactly the way Kanji is drawn (not necessarily every time). Let us have a look at it.

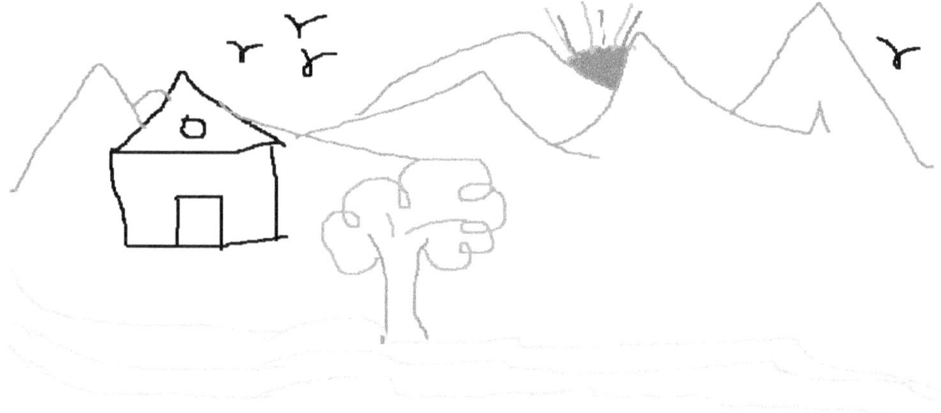

Well, I am not much sharp at drawings, but this helped me while learning Japanese. Observe the river in the above picture carefully. Now I will simply cut some portion of that river and will align it vertically.

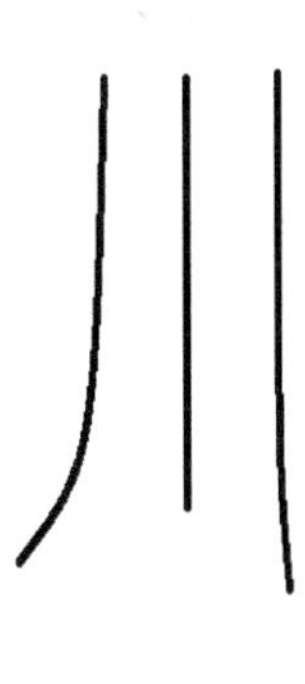

Pic. 1   Pic. 2

The symbol is shown in Pic. 2 represents Kanji for 'river' 川, which is pronounced as 'kawa' .'Likewise, Kanji for a tree is - 木, which is pronounced as 'ki'. Kanji for home, i.e., 'Uchi' or 'i.e.' is 家.

Thus, every Kanji has its distinct meaning.

Every Kanji has two readings, namely Kun-Yomi and on-Yomi. Kun -Yomi is the Japanese pronunciation assigned to the character (Kanji), and on-Yomi is the Chinese pronunciation retained by it.

For e.g., This Kanji has two readings.

Japanese reading – kunyomi – kawa- かわ

Chinese reading – onyomi – sen⏌ セン

When the complete word is written using only a combination of two or more Kanjis, the word is read using its on-yomi is preferred. But if the word is a combination of Hiragana and Kanjis, then its Kun-Yomi reading is preferred. But this is not always true. (This is applicable in 95% of cases, and yet 5% exceptions are there. To overcome this hurdle, you have to achieve fluency in Japanese. You need to gain in vocabulary.)

In the subsequent chapters, we will discuss a few of the Kanjis in depth. Let us understand Hiragana, the basic script in Japanese and the easiest one.

<u>Hiragana</u>

To represent particles in grammar and in the quest of having its own language, Hiragana was created. Hiragana is created using a few parts of Kanjis. Rather, we can take it as a simplified version of Kanjis.

About Hiragana-

Hiragana consists of 46 basic letters.

Adding two dots at the right head side of a letter is known as dakuten, and adding a circular symbol is known as han-dakuten. These symbols modify the utterance of that letter, and thus these newly formed letters are known as modifiers. They are modified versions of Hiragana, thus known as modifiers.

Every letter has a different pronunciation.

Hiragana is used only for Japanese words. i.e., for native

While reading, there are certain rules, such as the double consonant effect contracted consonants which are to be followed. We will discuss the detailed Hiragana with rules to be followed while reading in subsequent chapters.

Katakana

Katakana script gets used for mentioning foreign words. Katakana follows all the same rules as Hiragana. Katakana also consists of 46 basic letters and 25 modifiers. The only difference between Hiragana and Katakana is in their writing systems. Katakana letters are written with short, sharp, and straight strokes, while Hiragana letters get characterized by their blunt and curved strokes. This is all you need to know about the three scripts of Japanese for now.

Chapter 1: Hiragana Scripts & Vocabulary

The salient points to remember while writing Hiragana is proper strokes and stroke order. Hiragana consists of:

5 – Vowels.

40 – Consonants.

1 – Nasal sound.

All the letters of Hiragana have their peculiar pronunciations. We will learn all the letters, stroke orders, and correct pronunciations step by step.

1st stroke	2nd stroke	3rd stroke	Letter	Representation (Pronunciation)	Story to memorize the letter
ー	す	あ	あ	a(aa)	Observe the letter keenly. It seems like a person is standing, and suddenly, a snake starts climbing on his body. What will he do in this case? Of course, he will shout as, "aa, help me! Save me!" And likewise, you can remember this pronunciation and script for this first letter - あ.
し	い		い	i(ee)	In Indian villages, noodles are not a habitual food type. So, in childhood, whenever I used to visit my granny's place and eat noodles with a fork, she used to say, "Ee, what are you eating? Is that earthworm? (This is a non-veg food).

					Don't eat it." And it helped me to remember this letter - い.
ゝ	う		う	u(oo)	An artist represents a heart as, ♡ _ ♡ ---- If this heart is divided into two equal parts, the right half is used to write this letter - う.
ゝ	え	え	え	E	This letter looks like 'Z' written using a calligraphy way of writing and a stroke on the head side - え.
⌣	お	お	お	o	This letter looks like 'aa' but there is a small change between aa and o. A stroke is there in letter o - お.

Now, let us learn a few words using these first five vowels. Practice them with pronunciation as pronunciation also plays a crucial role in this language.

Maintain a separate diary to write these newly added words to your vocabulary.

<u>Word – Pronunciation – meaning</u>

あい – ai – love

あう – au – to meet

いい – ii – good

いう – iu – to say, to declare

いえ – ie – home

いいえ – iie – no

うえ – ue – above

え – e – picture, drawing

あおい – aoi – blue

おおい – ooi – a lot of

Now practice these words. Write them in a notebook dedicated to new words and read them aloud.

1st stroke	2nd stroke	3rd stroke	4th stroke	Letter	Representation (Pronunciation)	Story to memorize the letter
つ	カ	か		か	Ka(kha)	If we observed this letter keenly, it exactly looks like the handle of a cup – **か**
ー	ニ	き	き	き	Ki(khi)	If we look at the key of a locker, it exactly looks like this 'ki.' When we learn the letters through imagination as I am displaying, then Japanese will start seeming like the easiest language. – **き**
く				く	Ku(khu)	This looks like the beak part of a bird, and a child

						generally calls every bird 'Kuku.' - く
い	に	け			け	Ke(khe)	This is simply an extended part of the letter i, which we learned in the set of the vowel. - け
	こ				こ	Ko(kho)	this looks like a horizontally aligned i, which we learned in the set of vowels. - こ

Key points to remember

• In Hiragana K-series, we represent it as 'ka,' but while pronouncing it, we have to pronounce it as 'Kha.'

• There is a little difference between the computer script and the handwritten letter, but the basic shape remains the same.

The words below are a combination of the first 10 letters that we have just learned.

Word – Pronunciation – meaning

あかい – Akai – red

あき – aki – autumn

いけ – ike – pond

いく – iku – to go

えき – eki – station

おく―oku – to put, to place

おおきい – ookii – big

かう―Kau – to buy

かお―Kao – face

き―ki – tree

こえ – koe – voice

ここ – Koko – here

Exercise –

Q. Name the following objects in Japanese. (Write in Hiragana)

1)

2)

3)

4)

5)

6)

7)

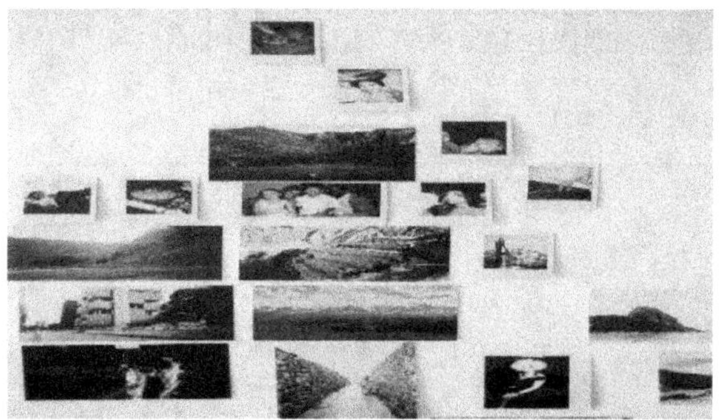

8)

Answers –

1. あかい – Red

2. かお - Face

3. いけ - Pond

4. あおい - Blue

5. き- Tree

6. えき - Station

7. いえ - Home

8. え - Pictures

Our third set of Hiragana letters is what is known as the S-series. S-series letters will be Sa, Shi, Su, Se, and So. Let us learn the next five letters of Hiragana.

1st stroke	2nd stroke	3rd stroke	Letter	Representation (Pronunciation)	Story to memorize the letter
﹁	さ	さ	さ	Sa	This letter is exactly similar to Ki, which we learned in K-series. The only difference is Sa has a single horizontal stroke, whereas Ki has two strokes. **Sa – さ.**
し			し	Shi	This looks like the handle of an Umbrella. It is a mirror image of J. **Shi – し**
一	す		す	Su	This letter looks like number two (2) written using curves and a single horizontal stroke. **Su – す**
一	ナ	せ	せ	Se	This letter can be better understood using the letter Ke. It looks like the left part of Ke (which we learned in K-Series) it is extended a little and thus

					we get a hint to memorize a new letter in Hiragana. **Se – せ**
ラ	そ		そ	So	It seems like, English letter Z in the upper half and C in the lower half are attached to each other in a calligraphic way of writing. Thus, this letter is easy to write and remember. **So - そ**

Practice writing these 15 letters as many times as you can. Practicing with perfect strokes is important. Now, this is time to add more vocabulary to our diary. Write and read aloud.

<u>Word – Pronunciation – meaning</u>

あさ – asa – Morning

あし – ashi – leg/foot

あそこ – asoko -- over there

いす – isu -- chair

おそく – osoku – late

おさけ – osake – alcohol

かさ – **Kasa -- an umbrella**

けさ — **kesa – this Morning**

さき — **saki – former, earlier**

し — **shi – four**

しお – **shio – salt**

しかし — **shikashi – but, however**

すき – **suki – like**

すこし – **sukoshi – a little**

おすし — **osushi – A very famous Japanese dish**

せかい – **Sekai – world**

そこ – **Soko – there**

How do you find it? Easy, isn't it? Just keep practicing. And it won't be difficult at all. More vocabulary and words are on the way. Enjoy learning the Japanese language.

We will now learn the next set of five letters. It's going to be fun learning these new letters and words. We'll soon be able to read short stories and conversations. Keep practicing and keep studying.

The next set of letters will be what is known as the T-series. It comprises of Ta, Chi, Tsu, Te, To. You should be careful about the two pronunciations of Chi and Tsu. They are not Ti and Tu. Let us take a look at these five letters.

1st stroke	2nd stroke	3rd stroke	4th stroke	Letter	Representation (Pronunciation)	Story to memorize the letter
ニ	ナ	だ	た	た	**Ta**	This letter has an A + shape symbol with ko-こ , which we learned in Ka –series ta- た.
ー	ち			ち	**Chi**	This letter exactly looks like a mirror image of the Sa-letter, which we learned in the S-series. The only difference between these two letters is the gap present in Sa isn't present in this letter. **Chi- ち.**
つ				つ	**Tsu**	**Do you still remember the heartbreak story, which I told you while learning the letter U- う? In that story, we were left with the left half part of a broken heart. That half part**

							we are going to utilize now. Take that left half part and align it horizontally. You will get this letter Tsu – つ.
て					て	Te	Observe this letter keenly. You will find that this letter is nothing but a horizontal line and an elongated C attached to it. Te- て.
と	と				と	To	This letter seems like the English letter y, written in a calligraphic way, drawing its lower half portion into the opposite side. This hint will work to remember this last letter of the Ta-series, To- と.

Thus now, we have a set of the first 20 letters of Hiragana. Let us now add a few more words to our vocabulary. Make sure you are practicing all the known words.

<u>Word – Pronunciation – meaning</u>

あした – Ashita – tomorrow

あたたかい – atatakai – warm

あつい – atsui – hot

いたい – itai – painful

いち – ichi – one

いつ – itsu – when

いつか – Itsuka – someday / fifth day of the month

いつつ – itsutsu – counter for five objects.

うた -- uta -- a song

うたう -- utau -- to sing

おとうと -- otouto -- younger brother

おとこ-- otoko -- male, man, guy

おととい -- ototoi -- the day before yesterday

おととし- ototoshi-- the year before last

かた-- kata --person(respect) / shoulder

きた -- Kita – North

くち -- kuchi – mouth

くつ -- kutsu – shoes

くつした - kutsushita – socks

こたえ – kotae – to answer, to reply

ことし – kotoshi – this year

さとう -- Satou – sugar

した -- shita -- under, down, below / tongue

しち – shichi – seven

そして -- soshite -- and then, thus

そと -- soto – outside

たいせつ -- taisetsu – important

たいてい -- taitei – mostly

たかい -- takai -- tall, high/expensive, costly

たつ - Tatsu -- to stand

ちいさい -- chiisai --small

ちち -- chichi -- father(own)

ついたち -- tsuitachi -- the first day of the month

つく -- tsuku -- to arrive, to reach

つき-- Tsuki -- the moon

つくえ -- tsukue – table

て -- te – hands

と -- to -- door / and, with

とおい -- tooi -- far, distant, far away

とおか - tooka -- the tenth day of the month

とけい -- tokei -- clock, watch

I'm damn sure you are finding things easy. If not, then it is simply a matter of some more practice. Keep practicing, and you will be dealing with these words with much ease.

NOTE - In the above words, while writing their meanings '/,' this punctuation is used many times. It is used to mention that many of the words having the same pronunciation might differ in their meanings. This is because every other word has different Kanji, but while writing in Hiragana, it might be the case of the same letters and pronunciation. To surpass this hurdle, we need to gain vocabulary. Also, with timely study, we will have command over Kanjis. Thus, we will be able to understand Japanese more precisely and appropriately. Keep practicing, and let us together put one more step towards being a master of this language.

It is surely an achievement to know 20 letters out of a total of 46 letters. Almost 50 % it is. Keep going. Perfect practice will bring perfect results.

Let us move to something more interesting than just writing Hiragana, a Japanese script. あいさつ、yes you read it correctly. It is aisatsu, which means greetings and salutations.

<u>Greeting's activity - Daily needed あいさつ</u>

Japan isn't only about three writing scripts, but it is the country of ethics, etiquettes, addressing someone with respect, punctuality are few of the たいせつ things every Japanese person takes care of. Now, as you all are learning Japanese, we all must know these greetings their etiquettes, and we have to implement these good habits as well.

This will not only be a lesson but also an exercise. Here, in this part, the pronunciation of greetings will be provided to you. You have to try to write its respective Hiragana below it.

Good morning -- Ohayou -- casual or informal

お＿＿＿う

Hello -- Konnichiwa -- Good afternoon/ -- Konnichiwa

こち

Good evening -- Konbanwa -- Casual or informal

こ＿＿＿＿＿

Good night -- Oyasumi -- casual or informal

お＿す＿＿

Good night Oyasuminasai -- polite or formal

お＿す＿さい

These are the most used greetings in everyday life. You also use it practically and believe me. It will not sound difficult anymore. Listen to the sounds of the phrases through the audiobook. When it comes to literature or a new language, writing, listening, and reading, all three of them have different aspects. When studying with the help of a book, you will only understand its writing part, but listening to it will clear all your doubts, and also your brain will get used to listening to these newly introduced words and syllables.

NOTE - If you have already listened to the audiobook, you might have come across a doubt of reading. We learned the letter す and practiced it to pronounce it as 'Su,' but in the greetings, we don't pronounce it as 'gozaimasu' but as 'gozaimas .'This word gozaimasu adds politeness and formality. While greeting family members or good friends, we can use short forms, but while greeting a teacher, boss or supervisor, always use gozaimasu as it is more polite and formal.

Our fifth set of Hiragana letters is the Na -series. The Na-series letters will be Na, Ni, Nu, Ne, and No. Let us learn the next five letters of Hiragana.

1st stroke	2nd stroke	3rd stroke	4th stroke	Letter	Representation (Pronunciation)	Story to memorize the letter
一	ナ	六	な	な	Na	This letter may remind you of one we have already learned. Yes. This is correct because this letter looks like ta – た, which we learned in the last letters. The only difference between these letters is the spring-like structure instead of Ko- こ.

い	じ	に		に	Ni	If you are studying regularly, you will find this letter is nothing but a combination of two letters, i.e., the left half of the letter **i – い** and the letter **ko - こ**. Thus, this letter is also straightforward to memorize. **Ni-に.**
い	ぬ			ぬ	Nu	The left half of the letter **i –い** and a girl with a pony, doing yoga helps to memorize this letter. If observed from the left, that large loop looks like a lap of that girl, and she is bending through her waist. While touching her head to the ground, the pony is coming downside. This imagination will help to memorize the letter **Nu – ぬ.**
J	オ	ね		ね	Ne	A straight line, 7 – like structure on the left side, and letter R – in calligraphic style on the right side, gives us a new letter

						from Hiragana, **Ne – ね.**
の				の	No	If the number 9 is drawn horizontally, it will look like this letter. This helps to remember the letter **No –の**.

Isn't it easy with imagination to memorize all these letters? If yes, then keep going. If not, then study a little more and develop your own ideas to memorize the letter. Someday, you might forget the letter, but these tricks will help you to remember these letters throughout your life.

<u>Word – Pronunciation – meaning</u>

あに – ani – elder brother

あね – ane – elder sister

あの – ano – that over there

いぬ – inu – dog

おかね – okane – money

おとな – otona – adult, grown-up

おなか – onaka – stomach, belly

きのう – kinou – yesterday

かない – kanai – wife

さかな – sakana – fish

この – kono – this

くに – kuni – country

しぬ – shinu – to die

その – sono – that

たのしい – tanoshii – enjoyable, fun

なか – naka – inside

なく – naku –to cry / to sing(bird)

なつ – natsu – summer

ななつ – nanatsu – seven

なに – nani – what

なな – nana – seven

なにか – nanika – something

なのか – nanoka – seventh day of the month

に – ni – two

にく -- niku – flesh, meat

にし – nishi – west

にち – niche – day

ねこ – neko – cat

This is the set of a few more words. Keep practising these words. Soon we will learn statement formation and will start with the grammar.

Exercise –

As you now know a decent amount of vocabulary and also a few of the letters from Hiragana, let us do an exercise.

Q.1. Fill in the blanks with the appropriate Hiragana.

Dog – __ぬ

Table – つ____

Day – ____

Tomorrow – あ__た

Seven – __ち

The tenth day of the month – とお__

Summer – な__

Money – お____

Elder brother – あ__

Meat – __く

to stand – た__

one – い__

morning – あ__

warm – あた____い

year before last – おと____

face – か__

chair – い__

salt – __お

autumn – ____

foot –あ__

A very famous Japanese dish –　お__し

Umbrella –　か__

Moon –　つ__

Shoes –　__つ

Big –　おお____

Sugar –　さ__う

Hands –　__

Tongue –し__

Something –　な__か

Small –　ちい__い

Make sure that you are writing all these words in your notebook as well.

Q.2. Match the pair.

なか	good
さき	door
いけ	earlier
うえ	painful
あおい	mouth
いく	north
せかい	male

いたい	the day before yesterday
おとこ	blue
あかい	pond
いい	above
おととい	world
きた	song
くち	inside
うた	to go
と	red

<u>Answers –</u>

Q.1

1.いぬ　2.つくえ　3.にち　4.あした　5.しち　6.とおか　7.なつ　8.おかね

9.あに　10.にく　11.たつ　12.いち　13.あさ　14.あたたかい　15.おととし

16.かお　17.いす　18.しお　19.あき　20.あし　21.おすし　22.かさ　23.つき

24.くつ　25.おおきい　26.さとう　27.て　28.した　29.なにか　30.ちいさい

Q.2

1. なか – inside	6. いく – to go	11. いい – good
2. さき – earlier	7. せかい – world	12. おととい - the day before yesterday
3. いけ – pond	8. いたい – painful	13. きた – north
4. うえ – above	9. おとこ – male	14. くち – mouth
5. あおい – blue	10. あかい – red	15. うた - song
16. と - door		

Let us now move to the next set of letters. This set contains letters from Ha – series. But these letters will not be Ha, Hi, Hu, He, and Ho, but will be Ha, Hi, Fu, He, and Ho. It might create confusion in the letters Ta, Na, and Ha. There is a very small difference while writing these letters. Thus keep an eye on their tricks and keep practising. Read aloud and write as many times as you can.

Ha – series letters.

1st stroke	2nd stroke	3rd stroke	4th stroke	Letter	Representation (Pronunciation)	Story to memorize the letter
し	し	は		は	Ha	The left half of letter i - い, a + number 9 taken horizontally, altogether gives us letter **Ha- は.**
ひ				ひ	Hi	Take a break and smile while uttering Hi, and you will find that a smiling face has this letter **Hi – ひ** from Hiragana.
ヽ	ろ	ふ	ふ	ふ	Fu	This letter looks like the English letter S, written in a calligraphic way and surrounded by three checkmarks,

						provides us with the letter **Fu – ふ.**
ヘ				ヘ	He	The water image of a checkmark with a sharp corner provides us with the new letter from Hiragana, i.e., the letter **He – ヘ.**
			ほ	ほ	Ho	This letter resembles the letter Ha-, which we learned at the beginning of the Ha - series. The only dissimilarity we get to spot in the letter Ha and Ho is an extra horizontal stroke is used in the Hiragana letter **Ho – ほ**

Let us move to more vocabulary now. These words will consist of all twenty-five letters, which we have learned till now. Write these words in the notebook and also read aloud. Make a habit of using these words in your daily routine so that they will be familiar to you.

<u>Word – Pronunciation – meaning</u>

は – ha – tooth

はい – hai – yes

はく – haku – to put on lower body clothes / to sweep, to clean

はこ – hako -- box

はし – Hashi – chopsticks/bridge

はた – hata – flag

はたち – hatachi – 20 years old (age 20 years)

はち – hachi – eight

はつか – hatsuka – 20th day of the month

はな – hana – flower/nose

はなし – hanashi – talk, conversation, speech

はは – haha – mother

はたけ – hatake – field

はと – hato – pigeon, dove

ひ – hi – day

ひく – hiku – to pull, to drawback/ to play instruments

ひくい – hikui – low, deep, short

ひな – hina – baby birds

ひこうき – hikouki – airplane

ひと – hito – person

ひとつ – hitotsu – for one thing, only, just

ひとつき – hitotsuki – one month

ふく－fuku – clothes / good luck, fortune / to wipe / to blow

ふたつ – futatsu -- for counting of two thing

ふつか – futsuka – the second day of the month

ふとい – futoi – fat, thick

へた – heta – poor at something

ほか – hoka – other

ほし – hoshi – star

ほしい – hoshii -- wanted, wished for

ほそい – hosoi – thin, slender

Let us move to the seventh set of letters of Hiragana. This set consists of consonants such as Ma, Mi, Mu, Me, and Mo. Sounds very easy, right? These will be the easiest to write and understand as well. But, make sure before moving to the next set of letters you are ready with good fluency in the last thirty letters.

1st stroke	2nd stroke	3rd stroke	4th stroke	Letter	Representation (Pronunciation)	Story to memorize the letter
一	二	ま		ま	Ma	Two horizontal strokes, one straight line, and a horizontally aligned number 9, altogether makes this letter the easiest to remember. Ma – ま.
み	み			み	Mi	In the Marathi language, Ma is written as म, so if this letter is written in a calligraphic way, we will get something that

							looks like the Japanese letter, Mi –み.
一	む	む			む	Mu	this resembles an extended letter Su –す, from Hiragana with a stroke, giving us this new letter, Mu – む.
㇀	め				め	Me	Well, this letter might be known to you. Check Na-series again. This letter looks like a reduced form of the letter Nu – ぬ, isn't it? To memorize this difference between these two letters, remember this story. We all love eating. Whenever we visit a hotel, firstly they provide us with a MeNu card. i.e. めぬ、thus this trick will help you to memorize these two letters with the dissimilarity

						present between them.
ニ	ニ	も		も	Mo	Letter Shi - し, from Hiragana with two horizontal strokes helps to understand this new letter Mo - も.

How is it going with acquiring knowledge of about the 35 letters of Hiragana and knowing many of the related words? I'm sure that you are enjoying it. Learning is the process to be enjoyed. Don't rush. Just go with the flow, and you will be doing amazing. Let us add a few more words to our vocabulary.

Word – Pronunciation – meaning

あたま – atama – head

あまい – amai – sweet

あめ – ame – rain

いつも – itsumo – always

いま – ima – now

いみ – imi – meaning

いもうと – imouto – younger sister

おとこのこ – otokonoko – boy

おみせ – omise – shop

おもい – omoi – heavy

かみ – kami – paper/hair

さむい – samui – cold

します – shimasu – do

すいます – suimasu – breathe

せまい – semai – narrow

たちます – tachimasu – stand

たてもの — tatemono – building

たのみます – tanomimasu – ask, request

つめたい – tsumetai – cold

つきます – tsukimasu – arrive

つけます – tsukemasu – turn on

つとめます – tsutomemasu – work for

とても – totemo – a lot, very

なまえ – namae – name

にもつ – nimotsu – luggage

ねます – nemasu – sleep

のむ – nomu – to drink

のみます – nomimasu – drink

のみもの – nomimono – beverages

はなします – hanashimasu – talk, speak

ひま – hima – free time

まいあさ – maiasa – every Morning

まいつき – maitsuki -- every month

まいにち – mainichi – every day

まいとし – maitoshi -- every year

まえ – mae – before

また – mata – again

まち – machi -- a city

まちます – machimasu – wait

みせます – misemasu – show

みち – michi – way

みなみ – minami – south

みます – mimasu -- see

みみ – mimi – ear

むいか – muika – the sixth day of the month

むこう – mukou – over there

め – me – eyes

もう – mou – again

もしもし – Hello (on-call)

もちます – mochimasu – hold

もの – mono – things

NOTE – Verbs, which will be read as suimasu, tachimasu, tsukimasu must be read as suimas, tachimas, and tsukimas respectively.

Now, we have a vast vocabulary in Japanese. Let us move to a very interesting activity. Keep studying all the words, make a habit of writing these words. Perfect practice done by you will ultimately be fruitful.

Exercise –

Q.1. Write the meanings of the words given below in Hiragana. Also, write its pronunciation.

1. things
2. way
3. city
4. east
5. west
6. south
7. boy
8. every year
9. very
10. narrow
11. box
12. head
13. eyes
14. ears
15. hair
16. seven
17. eight
18. stomach
19. every day

20. month

21. first day of the month

22. Sixth day of the month

23. star

24. cold

25. nose

26. always

27. inside

28. earlier

29. Painful

30. table

Q.2. Identify the following images and write their names in Japanese.

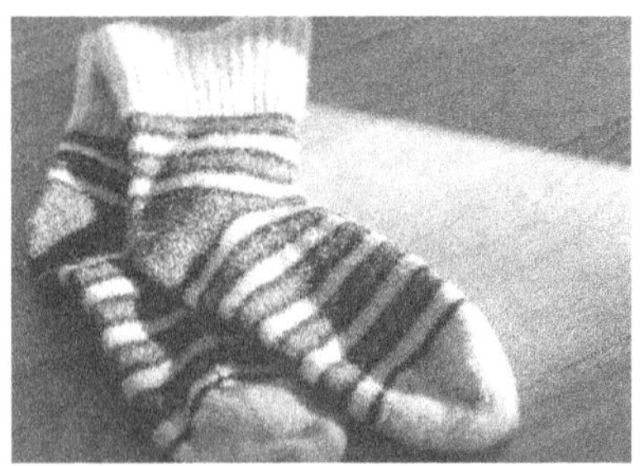

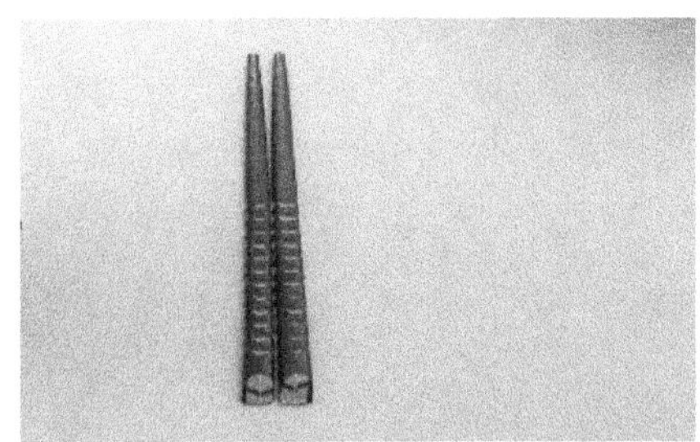

Q.3 Fill in the blanks.

1. さ＿な -- Fish

2. な＿ -- inside

3. おさ＿ – Japanese alcohol

4. ち＿ -- father

5. か＿＿＿ -- wife

6. に＿＿＿ -- luggage

7. の＿もの -- beverages

8. た＿い -- expensive

9. ほそ＿ – thin, slender

10. まい＿＿＿ – every day

11. お＿い -- heavy

12. い＿も -- always

13. し＿す -- do

14. おか＿ -- money

15. くつ＿た – socks

16. い＿う＿ – younger sister

17. あ＿ elder sister

18. おと＿の＿ – boy

19. な＿え -- name

20. こた＿ – to answer

21. ね＿ – cat

22. は＿け – field

23. あ＿た – tomorrow

24. おお＿い – ookii

25. ち＿さ＿ – small

26. す＿し – a little

27. ＿まい – narrow

28. き＿う – yesterday

29. せ＿い – world

30. ふ＿＿＿ – fat, thick

31. い＿ – chair

32. ＿お – face

Answers –

Q.1.

1.ほん　2. くつした　3. かわ　4. たてもの　5.はし　6.すし・おすし　7.はな

8.ねこ　9. いぬ　10.つき

Q.2.

1.さかな　2. なか　3. おさけ　4.ちち　5.かない　6.にもつ　7.のみもの　8.たかい

9.ほそい　10. まいにち　11.おもい　12.いつも　13.します　14.おかね　15.くつした

16.いもうと　17.あね　18.おとこのこ　19.なまえ　20.こたえ　21.ねこ　22.はたけ

23.あした　24.おおきい　25.ちいさい　26.すこし　27.せまい　28.きのう　29.せかい

30.ふとい　31.いす　32.かお

Let us now move to the next set of letters. The 8th set of letters consists of only three letters, Ya, Yu, and Yo, respectively. Letter Yi sounds equivalent to I, and letter Ye sounds equivalent to e. Thus, they are not included in the Ya-series. Let us learn these letters with stroke order and with memory tricks.

1st stroke	2nd stroke	3rd stroke	Letter	Representation (Pronunciation)	Story to memorize the letter
や	や	や	や	Ya	A half of S letter aligned horizontally, a cross line and a stroke altogether gives us a letter, Ya – や.
ゆ	ゆ		ゆ	Yu	If you observed it keenly, you will notice that this looks like half left of the letter i -い, and a mirror image of number 9 when taken horizontally. With an addition of a concave mirror shape (curved line), we get this letter Yu – ゆ.
よ	よ		よ	Yo	The commonly used part in letter Ha-は, Na-な, and Ma – ま with a horizontal stroke gives us the letter Yo – よ.

Now we have a set of 38 letters with us and also have a decent vocabulary with us. Adding vocabulary is an endless process. In order to achieve fluency in Japanese, we have to keep learning. We have to keep studying. Write down the following vocabulary in your notebook. Don't forget to read aloud while writing.

<u>Word – Pronunciation – meaning</u>

やおや – yaoya – vegetable store

やさい – yasai – vegetable

やさしい – yasashii – easy, gentle

やすい – yasui – inexpensive, cheap

やすみ – yasumi – holiday, vacation

やすみます – yasumimasu – have a day off, rest

やま – yama – mountain

ゆうめい – yuumei – famous

ゆき – yuki – snow

ようか – youka – the eight day of the month

ようふく – youfuku – western clothes

よく – yoku – often

つよい – tsuyoi – strong

よこ – yoko --- the side

よむ – yomu – to read

たいよう – taiyou – sun

はやく – hayaku – early, soon, quickly

やきとり – yakitori – grilled chicken

へや – heya – room

いや – iya – unpleasant, disagreeable

おや – oya – parents

Let us move ahead with the ninth set of Hiragana letters. This set consists of the Ra – series. The letters are Ra, Ri, Ru, Re, and Ro, respectively.

1st stroke	2nd stroke	3rd stroke	Letter	Representation (Pronunciation)	Story to memorize the letter
ﾞ	ら		ら	Ra	The lower half part of number 5 with a stroke above altogether gives us the letter Ra -ら.
l	り		り	Ri	The left half of the letter i –い, with a right half of a broken heart helps us write the letter Ri – り.
る			る	Ru	This looks similar to number 3 with a curve in the lower half. This will help to remember this letter Ru -る.
J	オ	れ	れ	Re	If observed keenly, this letter looks like a straight line with the number 7 in a calligraphic way on its left and a water image of the letter S on its right half. It will give us the letter Re - れif drawn in a calligraphic way.
ろ			ろ	Ro	Number 3 drawn in a calligraphic way gives us the letter Ro – ろ. Mark the difference between the letter Ru-る and Ro -ろ.

Including this, we now have a total of 43 letters. With these letters, let us now add more vocabulary to our knowledge. Write and read aloud.

Word – Pronunciation – meaning

あちら – achira – that way

あたらしい – atarashii – new

あまり – Amari – not much

あります – arimasu – exist, be, have

あるきます – arukimasu – to walk

あれ – are – that over there

いくら – ikura – how much?

います – irimasu – to be needed, necessary, must have

いれます – iremasu – put in

いろ – iro -- color

いろいろ – iroiro -- various

うしろ – ushiro – back, behind

うまれます – umaremasu – be born

うる – uru – to sell

うります – urimasu -- sell

うるさい – urusai -- loud

うれしい – ureshii – happy, pleased

おてあらい – otearai -- toilet

おります – orimasu – get off, get down

からい – karai – hot, spicy

かります – karimasu -- borrow

かるい – karui – light, not heavy

きいろい – kiiroi -- yellow

くもり – kumori – cloudy weather

くるま – kuruma -- car

くろい – kuroi -- black

こちら – kochira – this way

こまります – komarimasu – to be in trouble

これ – kore – this

しめる – shimeru -- close

しります – shirimasu – know, be aware of

しろい – shiroi – white

そら – sora – sky

それ – sore – that

それから – sorekara – and then, after that

とり – tori -- bird

とりにく – toriniku – chicken, meat

となり – tonari – next to, adjoining, adjacent

ぬります – nurimasu – paint, plaster

のります – norimasu – get on train, bus, etc.

はる – haru -- spring

はれ – hare – clear weather

ひる – hiru – afternoon, midday

ひろい – hiroi – spacious, wide

ふります – furimasu – fall rain, snow etc.

ふるい – furui – old, aged

ふろ – furo -- bath

まるい– marui -- circle

もらいます – moraimasu -- receive

ろく – roku – six

Having a set of around 43 letters and having so many words in our vocabulary is truly an achievement. Keep practising. We have to be the best in Japanese. To achieve it, we have to keep on practising. The more we will learn, the more we will grow. Let us make it easiest. The following successive activities will help you to memorize these words.

Exercise –

`Q.1.Identify these images presented below and fill in the blanks accordingly.

1.

お＿＿＿す

2.

ま＿＿＿

3.

た＿よ＿

4.

＿つ

5.

い＿

6.

＿な

7.

のみ＿の

8.

＿のし＿

9.

さ＿な

10.

＿める

11.

つま＿な＿

12.

＿こう＿

1.おります   2. まるい   3.   たいよう   4.くつ   5.いす   6.ひな   7.のみもの   8.たのしい   9.っさかな
10.しめる   11.つまらない   12.ひこうこ

The next and last set of Hiragana consists of only three letters. This set is very important and a little different from other sets of Hiragana. This series includes letters Wa, Wo, and n.

1st stroke	2nd stroke	3rd stroke	Letter	Representation (Pronunciation)	Story to memorize the letter
Ｊ わ			わ	Wa	A straight line, number 7 on the left side, and a mirror image of C altogether gives us the letter Wa – わ.
ー ち	を		を	Wo	Observe the letter properly. A horizontal line, the English alphabet h drawn in a calligraphic way and the number 8 is written as ८ in the Marathi language, thus all these shapes help us to remember this letter Wo – を.
ん				ん	n-vowel	This letter is parallel to the English alphabet h. Letter n – ん.

As this letter is written as n-vowel. It helps us to produce a nasal sound n. Thus, this letter is used in many words. With the help of the words presented below, you will understand the proper use of this letter. Keep studying and keep practising. But keep a point in mind, even though I said that Hiragana consists of 46 letters, this is not the end of the Hiragana. Something is yet to come into the picture. Practice the words below.

<u>Word – Pronunciation – meaning</u>

おにいさん – oniisan – elder brother

おねえさん – oneesan – elder sister

おかあさん – okaasan – someone's mother

おとうさん – otousan – someone's father

さん – san – three

おんな – onna – female

おんなのこ – onnanoko -- a girl

かんたん – kantan -- easy

しつもん – shitsumon – question, inquiry

せん – sen -- thousand

せんたく – sentaku – washing clothes

たいへん – taihen – serious, difficult

たくさん – takusan – a lot, many

てんき – tenki -- weather

なん – nan – what

なんにち – nannichi – what day

ほん – hon -- book

ほんとう – hontou – truth, reality

ほんや – honya – book store

みんな – minna – all, everyone, everybody

みかん – mikan – orange

もん – mon – gate

まん – man – ten thousand

らいねん – rainen – next year

わかい – wakai – young, youthful

かわいい – kawaii – cute, adorable

わかります – wakarimasu -- understand

わたります – watarimasu – cross over, go across

わるい – warui – bad, undesirable, poor

わすれる – wasureru – to forget

わたし – watashi – I

わたくし – watakushi – I (formal)

わたす – watasu – to hand over, to pass /to carry across

わかもの – wakamono – young man, young woman, youngster

わし – washi -- eagle

わた – wata – cotton

わに – wani – crocodile

We have now completed all the 46 letters of basic Hiragana. Now, this is the time to learn a little more about the script Hiragana itself. Extended Hiragana is nothing but a combination of basic Hiragana and Modifiers. In order to learn these modifiers, we need to know a few things. Let us move to a new concept called Modifiers.

SPECIAL BONUS

Want this bonus book for **FREE**?

Get **FREE**, unlimited access to it and all of my new books by joining the fan base

Scan with phone to join!

Chapter 2: Modifiers

With slight modification in a few of the letters from the Hiragana script, we get a different phonetic sound. These modified letters of Hiragana are known as Modifiers.

1. Adding two dots to the letter is known as dakuten. i.e. {"}

2. It changes the pronunciation of these series,

From	To
か - ka	が - ga
さ- sa	ざ - za
た - ta	だ - da
は - ha	ば - ba

1. Also, adding a small circular symbol is known as Han-dakuten.

2. It changes the pronunciation of Ha-series to Pa-series.

は ----> ぱ

Let us look in detail at this modifier table.

Modifier chart

ga - series	za - series	da - series	ba - series	Pa - series
が ga	ざ za	だ da	ば ba	ぱ pa
ぎ gi	じ ji	ぢ ji	び bi	ぴ pi
ぐ gu	ず zu	づ zu	ぶ bu	ぷ pu
げ ge	ぜ ze	で de	べ be	ぺ pe
ご go	ぞ zo	ど do	ぼ bo	ぽ po

This is the set of twenty-five Modifiers. Thus, including all these modifiers, we have a total of 71 letters, and altogether they are known as Hiragana. Let us add a few words to our dictionary consisting of these modifiers. Don't cease your practice. Keep in mind that more concepts are on the way. The more we have acquaintance with the prior concepts, the easier it will be to understand new concepts.

Word – Pronunciation – meaning

あがる – agaru – to go up

あげる – ageru – to give

あさごはん – asagohan – breakfast

あびる – abiru – to take a shower

あそぶ – asobu – to play

あぶない – abunai – dangerous

いそがしい – isogashii -- busy

いちど – ichido – once

いりぐち – iriguchi – entrance

えいが – eiga – movie

えいがかん – eigakan – movie theatre

えいご – eigo – English language

えらぶ – erabu – to choose, to select

えんぴつ – enpitsu – pencil

おなじ – onaji -- same

おばさん – obasan -- aunt

おばあさん – obaasan -- grandmother

おべんとう – obentou – lunch box

おぼえる – oboeru – to memorize

かぜ – kaze -- wind

かぞく – kazoku -- family

かばん – kaban -- bag

かびん – kabin -- a vase

かがみ – kagami – mirror

かど – kato -- corner

ごご – koko – afternoon, p.m.

ごぜん – gozen – a.m.

ことば – kotoba -- words

ごはん – gohan – meal

こんげつ – kongetsu – this month

さいご – saigo -- end

さんぽ – sanpo – walk

しずか – shizuka -- silent

じぶん – jibun -- oneself

ぜんぶ – zenbu – all

そうじ – souji -- cleaning

そば – soba – near

みじかい – mijikai – short

だいがく – daigaku -- university

たべもの – tabemono -- food

たべます – tabemasu -- eat

てがみ – tegami -- letter

でんわ – denwa – telephone

ながい – nagai – long

ほんだな – hondana – bookshelf

ぼうし – boushi – hat

So, we have now completed Hiragana. However, there is something that we know as "extended hiragana"

Extended Hiragana consists of a few more letters. These are a few contracted consonants. There is also one of the concepts called 'double consonant' which is yet to be discussed. Let us move ahead towards these concepts.

Chapter 3: Double consonants & Contracted consonants

Till now we have learnt almost all the letters from Hiragana. Hiragana is truly very limited and thus easy to memorize. But what if the word to be written in Hiragana sounds like a double consonant?

Being fluent in Hiragana, including modifiers

I can write 'kitsupu,' but how do I write 'kippu'?

I can write 'kisatsuten' but how do I write 'kissaten'?

This is what the double consonant concept is. While writing kippu, kissaten, shippu, zasshi, and ikkai.

this concept helps us.

1. Generally, all the letters are of the same height in Hiragana. But, while writing a word with Hiragana, if small つ is used, it gives us the double consonant effect.

2. In that case, つ loses its own phonetic and gives rise to a new way of pronunciation.

3. Small つ duplicates the consonant used in the letter next to it.

Let us look into a few of the examples.

Normal つ	Small つ
きつぷ – kitsupu	きっぷ – kippu – ticket
きつさてん -- kitsusaten	きっさてん – kissaten – coffee shop
しつぷ – shitsupu	しっぷ – shippu – poultice
ざつし – zatsushi	ざっし – zasshi – magazine

But not the same case is repeated while writing double consonants using phonetic n. In that case, there is no need to use a small つ.

Onna – おんな – female

Gunmaken – ぐんまけん – Gunma prefecture

Onnanoko – おんあのこ – girl

Let us practice a few more words like this.

Word – Pronunciation – meaning

あさって – asatte – the day after tomorrow

がっこう – gakkou – school

きっさてん – kissaten – coffee shop

きって – kitte -- stamp

きっぷ – kippu – ticket

けっこん– kekkon – marriage

せっけん – sekken – soap

まっすぐ – massugu – straight(ahead)

みっか – mikka – the third day of the month

みっつ – mittsu – three things

むっつ – muttsu – six things

もっと – motto – more

ゆっくり – yukkuri – slowly, unhurriedly

よっつ – yottsu – four things

りっぱ – rippa – splendid, fines

This is how our vocabulary is increasing with more and more basic concepts. If we learn Japanese in this way, then it won't be as difficult as it seems. You just have to keep practising. Maintain consistency, and you will soon be fluent in Japanese.

Contracted consonants

1. Contracted consonant terms are related to い－ending consonants from Hiragana.

2. It is applicable to both basic Hiragana and modifiers as well.

3. Small や、ゆ、and よ are used in contracted consonants.

Let us learn all the contracted consonants in detail.

For e.g. き+や ---◊ きや – kiya

き+や -------◊きゃ – kya

The second case provides us with the concept of contracted consonants. Let us look into the chart of the contracted consonants.

Pronunciation	Letter	Pronunciation	Letter	Pronunciation	Letter
Kya	きゃ	Kyu	きゅ	Kyo	きょ
Sha	しゃ	Shu	しゅ	Sho	しょ
Cha	ちゃ	Chu	ちゅ	Cho	ちょ
Nya	にゃ	Nyu	にゅ	Nyo	にょ
Hya	ひゃ	Hyu	ひゅ	Hyo	ひょ
Mya	みゃ	Myu	みゅ	Myo	みょ
Rya	りゃ	Ryu	りゅ	Ryo	りょ
Gya	ぎゃ	Gyu	ぎゅ	Gyo	ぎょ
Jya	じゃ	Jyu	じゅ	Jyo	じょ
Bya	びゃ	Byu	びゅ	Byo	びょ
Pya	ぴゃ	Pyu	ぴゅ	Pyo	ぴょ

Here you have crossed a very important milestone towards learning Japanese. Let us now add a few words to our vocabulary. This contracted consonant's part will be discussed in these words. Make sure you know the whole of the Hiragana before practising these words. Writing practice is as essential as the practice of reading.

Word – Pronunciation – meaning

いっしょ – issho – together

きゅう – kyuu – nine

きょうしつ – kyoushitsu – classroom

きょう – kyou – today

きょうだい – kyoudai – siblings, brother, and sister

きょうと – kyouto – Kyoto (the name of a city in Japan)

きょねん – kyonen – last year

ぎゅうにゅう – gyuunyuu – cow's milk

しゃしん – shashin – photograph

しゅう – shuu – week

じゅう – juu -- ten

じゅぎょう — jugyou – class, lesson

しゅくだい – shukudai – homework

じょうず – jouzu – skillful, good at

じょうぶ – joubu – healthy, strong

しょうゆ – shouyu – soy sauce

しょくどう — shokudou – dining room, dining hall

たんじょうび – daijoubi – birthday

だいじょうぶ – daijoubu – alright, OK, OK

ちょうど – choudo – precisely, just

ちょっと – chotto – a little, a bit

としょかん – toshokan – library

びょういん – byouin -- hospital

まいしゅう – maishuu – every week

にんぎょう – ningyou – doll, puppet

りゅうがくせい – ryuugakusei – a student studying abroad

りょうしん – ryoushin – parents

りょうり – ryouri – cooking

りょこう – ryokou – travel, trip

Let us solve an exercise now. It will surely help you to remember the words we have discussed till now. All you need to do is try to memorize all the words learnt till now. It will surely be very interesting to learn a few more concepts of the Japanese language.

<u>Exercise –</u>

Q.1 Answer the following in Japanese.

1. Tell me the color of human tooth ----

2. The size of the hulk is ----

3. The length of a snake compared to an earthworm is ----

4. The shape of the sun is ----

5. In nature, we get fruits from ---

6. The famous dish of Japan is ---

7. Japanese lunch box –

8. The shelf on which books can be stored is ----

9. Colour of hair, in general, is ----

10. When we are sick, we visit ----

Q.2 Fill in the blanks.

1. A chef is _______ at cooking –

2. A singer can be ______at cooking –

3. Everyone collects money for _____ tour –

4. We visit _____ to read and exchange books –

5. In the nighttime, the ____ is full of moon and stars –

6. We put _____ on our head –

7. ______ is a flying vehicle with fixed wings –

8. We visited _______ with my friends to have a cup of coffee –

9. Every Morning I take a bath using _______ --

10. After my bath, I get ready and comb my hair, looking into the ______ --

11. Everyone puts on a lovely _____ before going to a ceremony –

12. In office hours, my father is very ________ --

13. We have to learn many _______ in order to be fluent in Japanese –

14. My mother is very _______ at heart –

15. In Japan _____ is used to eat food –

<u>Answers</u> –

Q.1

1. しろい　2. おおきい　3.　ながい　4. まるい　5. き　6.おすし
7.おべんとう　8. ほんだな　9. くろい　10.びょういん

Q.2

1.じょうず　2.へた　3. せかい　4.としょかん　5.そら　6.ぼうし　7.ひこうき
8.きっさてん　9. せっけん　10. かがみ　11.ふく　12.いそがしい　13.ことば
14.しんせつ　15. はし

<u>Hiragana Chart –</u>

	わ	ら	や	ま	は	な	た	さ	か	あ
		り		み	ひ	に	ち	し	き	い
		る	ゆ	む	ふ	ぬ	つ	す	く	う
		れ		め	へ	ね	て	せ	け	え
ん	を	ろ	よ	も	ほ	の	と	そ	こ	お

It is truly great to have such a huge vocabulary with us. Many interesting topics are about to come in subsequent chapters. Now, this is the time to move a little deep into the earlier part of あいさつ.

Chapter 4: Greetings - あいさつ

Let us complete those fill in the blanks from the topic **daily greetings** あいさつ.

Now we can fill in those blanks, which we left earlier.

Good morning --   Ohayou   -- casual or informal

     おはよう

 Good Morning - ohayou   gozaimasu   -- polite   or formal

     おはようございます

Good afternoon/ -- Konnichiwa

Hello   こんいちは

Good evening   -- Konbanwa

     こんばんは

Good night   -- Oyasumi   -- casual or informal

     おやすみ

     Oyasuminasai   -- polite   or formal

     おやすみなさい

NOTE – You might be noticing some highlighted parts above. As you all are practicing Hiragana, you might have thought that it was a typing error or a printing mistake. But, no. You read it right. Even though I have written Konnichiha in Japanese, I read it as Konnichiwa. This is because, when the noun letter は is read as Ha and when it acts as a grammar particle or a part of interjection, it is read as Wa. Thus, in this case, all these greetings are parallel to interjection. Thus, this change in pronunciation occurs. Even when this letter は acts as a topic marker in a statement, it is pronounced as Wa. We will learn in detail about this in further topics.

Thanking

While thanking someone, various ways are used to express gratitude towards someone. It depends upon whom you are bidding thanks. Likewise, the situation also matters.

どうぞ – douzo – please/please go ahead / please have it

どうも – doumo – thanks

ありがとう – arigatou – thanks (Informal or casual way)

どうもありがとう – doumo arigatou – thanks a lot

どうもありがとうございます – doumo arigatou gozaimasu – thank you very much

ありがとうございます – arigatou gozaimasu – thank you (polite)

どうもありがとうございました – doumo arigatou gozaimashita – thank you for what you have done. (Past tense of gozaimasu – gozaimashita is used.)

Douzo is generally used to offer things to someone or to invite them. We should never use short forms to our teacher, supervisor, boss, and senior.

Doumo expresses gratitude or apology. Thus, used with ありがとう（thanks and すみません（I'm sorry）. It enhances the intensity of gratitude or apology.

ございます indicates politeness and formality. In addition to this ございました indicates that the act has been completed.

<u>Apologizing</u>

While saying sorry, it again depends on if you are being sorry for what you are about to do or if you are sorry for what you have done. To whom you are saying sorry to your friend, colleague, sensei or boss and also the reason behind it. Let us learn to say sorry to someone. Sorry and thanks both are golden words, it shows that you're being polite towards people. Hence learn it properly.

すみません – sumimasen -- sorry (formal)

すみませんでした – sumimasen deshita -- sorry (formal)

ごめん – gomen – sorry (informal)

ごめんなさい – gomennasa –sorry (semi-formal, generally used when something very bad is done.)

もうしわけありません – moushiwake arimsen – I'm sorry, I feel regretful (business – native way)

すみません shows that you are saying sorry for what you are about to do. すみませんでした shows that you are being sorry for what has already happened. ごめん is a very informal way of saying sorry to family, friends. ごめんなさい is used when we have done something which is very bad. Generally, kids say sorry to their parents using this expression.

もうしわけありません is used in business, to say sorry. もうしわけない is also used instead of もうしわけありません.

Starting and Ending Eating/Drinking

いただきます – itadakimasu – (formal) ritual expression before having a meal

ごちいそいさま – gochisousama – (formal) ritual expression before having a meal

ごちそうさまでした - gochisousamadeshita - (formal) ritual expression before having a meal

かんぱい - kanpai - Cheers

いただきます has no exact translation into English, as it is a ritual expression. But it is equivalent to 'Thank you for the meal that you have just served' or 'I received'. ごちいそいさま is used just after having food. It means 'Thank you for the food that I ate' or 'I enjoyed my meal very much, thank you. かんぱい is used before having drinks in a celebration or in the honour of something.

Requesting or asking for something

すみません - sumimasen - excuse me.

おねがいします - onegaishimasu - （Humble）can you give it to me? / Please

____をおねがいします -- ____woonegaishimasu -- ____please give me. (Humble)

もういちどおねがいします - mou ichido onegaishimasu - One more time, please.

______をください -- ______wo kudasai - Please give me. (Respectful)

みずをください – mizu wo kudasai – please give me water.

みかんをください – mikan wo kudasai – Please, give me orange.

______ください -- ______ kudasai – Please do for me. (Respectful)

よんでください – yonde kudasai – Please read.

かいてください – kaite kudasai – Please write.

のんでください – nonde kudasai – please drink.

While answering these requests, you can answer as—

はいどうぞ – hai douzo – Sure, here you go.

<u>Entering into a room/leaving a room –</u>

Before entering into a room knock on the door twice,

ごめんください – gomen kudasai – May I come in?

Excuse me. Is anyone around?

ようこそ – youkoso – ritual expression to welcome someone to a place or home.

Welcome!

Nice to see you!

おじゃまします – ojamashimasu – (While entering into someone's home) Excuse me, for disturbing you.

おじゃましました – ojamashimashita – Sorry, I bothered you. (While leaving someone's home)

ごめんください is used while knocking on the door to ask as if someone is around. While entering into a room use greeting おじゃまします, which means 'I'm sorry because now I'm going to bother you for some time. おじゃましました is the past tense of おじゃまします, which means 'I'm sorry for what I have already done. ようこそ is used by the person who opens the door.

どうぞおはいりくださいください – douzo ohairi kudasai – Please come in.

<u>Leaving and Coming Back to Home –</u>

When someone enters the home, they use an expression.

ただいま – tadaima – I'm home.

Here I am.

The meaning of the word ただいま is presently, right away, just now. This word is also used in a few statements to mention that the task or activity has happened just now. But as a phrase or greeting it is used when someone reaches home.

In order to respond to, I'm home, the following phrase is used.

おかえりいなさい – okaerinasai – welcome back.

Welcome home.

While leaving home,

いってきます – ittekimasu – see you later.

I'm leaving.

いってらっしゃい – itterasshai – See you later.

Have a safe trip.

Have a good day.

Take care.

ただいま -- ritual expression upon coming home

おかえりいなさい – ritual response to tadaima

いってきます – ritual expression when leaving home

いってらっしゃい – ritual response to ittekimasu

<u>When meeting someone for the very first time –</u>

If you are meeting someone for the very first time, there is a specific greeting that is used.

はじめまして – hajimemashite – how are you doing?

I'm glad to meet you.

While initiating a conversation hajimemashite is used and at the end of the conversation, the following phrases are used.

よろしくおえがいします – yoroshiku onegaishimasu – please remember me.

Please treat me well.

I'm looking forward to working with you.

よろしくおねがいいたします – yoroshiku onegai itashimasu – (officially used instead of the above phrase)

どうぞよろしく – douzo yoroshiku – I'm pleased to meet you.

Please favour me.

よろしくおねがいいたします is used at the end of an Email, instead of よろしくおえがいします. よろしくおえがいします is used at the end of a conversation. It is also used in business meetings or group work in university.

Meeting People for the First Time –

When meeting a person for the very first time, we use the greeting 'hajimemashite'. Verbally the meaning of hajimemashite means to start, to begin, to commence. But it is also used as a ritual expression at the beginning of the self-introduction when you are meeting someone for the very first time. Thus, it pertains to meaning similar to 'How are you doing?' or 'nice to meet you.'

はじめまして – hajimemashite

At the end of the conversation, the greeting yoroshiku is used. Yoroshiku means 'thanks in advance.' But in order to add more politeness to this word, it is used with a few other words. The longer phrase show more politeness than the shorter one. Thus, the following greetings are used at the end of the conversation.

どうぞよろしく – douzo yoroshiku – pleased to meet you.

Thanks for your favours in advance.

よろしくおねがいします — yoroshiku onegaishimasu – pleased to meet you.

I look forward to working with you.

どうぞよろしくおねがいします – douzo yoroshiku onegaishimasu – business or official level

どうぞよろしくおねがいします has the same meaning as above but the level of politeness

increases. It is used when introducing yourself. As if introducing to a new company as an employee you will surely need some co-assistance from your colleagues, so it acts as a thank you in advance for all the help you are going to provide me with.

<u>Taking Leave or crossing someone's path –</u>

しつれいします – shitsureishimasu – Excuse me. (With a bow)

じゃしつれいします – ja shitsureishimasu – well, excuse me. (I'll take a leave then.)

This phrase is used when entering into someone's house or workplace. But the same is also used when passing in front of somebody. Having food with co-workers and phone rings, before taking your call shitsureishimasu is used. To excuse ourselves before doing something. Likewise, before leaving a place this is used.

おつかれさまです -- Otsukaresama desu – Before entering and after meeting

おつかれさまでした – otsukaresamadeshita – while leaving the workplace.

When you arrive at your workplace after your colleagues, you must bid them Otsukaresama desu. After coming back from a meeting, colleagues bid each other with Otsukaresama desu. When leaving office after work, you must bid others with the phrase 'otsukaresamadeshita' and your colleagues also wish the same. This phrase is used at the workplace to respect the work done by someone. It is also used casually with colleagues or with people with higher authority, to appreciate or to respect their work.

<u>Parting –</u>

おさきにしつれいします – osakini shitsureishimasu – Excuse me for leaving first.

If you finished your work and leave the office before your colleagues, you must use this phrase.

またね – matane – see you later – casual

じゃまた – ja mata – well then see you again. – polite

じゃまたね – ja mata ne – well then see you later. (more polite)

さようなら – sayounara – good bye.

Chapter 5: Katakana

After Hiragana, the other script of Japanese used for non - Japanese words or from the transcription of words from foreign languages is Katakana. The best part about Katakana is it has got the same pronunciation as Hiragana. It is just different in the writing method. It consists of conical shapes. Go through the chart below.

Aa - series	ア	イ	ウ	エ	オ
Ka – series	カ	キ	ク	ケ	コ
Sa – series	サ	シ	ス	セ	ソ
Ta – series	タ	チ	ツ	テ	ト
Na - series	ナ	ニ	ヌ	ネ	ノ
Ha - series	ハ	ヒ	フ	ヘ	ホ
Ma - series	マ	ミ	ム	メ	モ
Ya – series	ヤ		ユ		ヨ
Ra – series	ラ	リ	ル	レ	ロ
Wa - series	ワ				ヲ
N-vowel					ン

<u>Similarities and differences between Hiragana and Katakana –</u>

1. Both have the same pronunciations.

2. The Writing script is different.

3. All the rules for modifiers, double consonant effect, contracted consonants, and pronunciation apply to both of them.

4. Katakana is used for the name of a country, a foreigner's name, and any foreign word which is transcribed into Japanese.

Let us discuss a few words in Katakana –

Word	pronunciation	meaning
アパート	apa-to	apartment
アメリカ	amerika	America
エアコン	eakon	air conditioner
エレベーター	erebe-ta-	elevator, lift
カタカナ	katakana	Katakana
カメラ	kamera	camera
カレンダー	karenda-	calendar
ギター	gita-	guitar
クラス	kurasu	class
ケーキ	ke-ki	cake
コート	ko-to	coat
コーヒー	ko-hi-	coffee
コップ	koppu	cup

コピー	kopi-	copy
サッカー	sakka-	soccer, football
シャツ	shatsu	shirt
シャワー	shawa-	shower
ジュース	jyusu	juice
ズボン	zubon	trouser, pants
スリッパ	surippa	slipers
セーター	se-ta-	sweater
ゼロ	zero	zero
タクシー	takushi-	taxi
テープ	te-pu	tape
テーブル	teburu	table
テスト	tesuto	test
デパート	depa-to	department
ドア	doa	door
トイレ	toire	toilet
トイレットペーパー	toirettope-pa-	toilet paper
ナイフ	naifu	knife

ニュース	nyu-su	news
ノート	no-to	notebook
バス	basu	bus
バター	bata-	butter
パン	pan	bread
ハンカチ	hankachi	handkerchief
ビル	biru	building
プール	pu-ru	pool, swimming pool
ボールペン	bo-rupen	Ball pen
ポケット	poketto	pocket
ボタン	botan	button
ホテル	hoteru	hotel
マッチ	macchi	match
メートル	me-toru	metre
ラーメン	ra-men	ramen, Chinese style noodles
ラジオ	rajio	radio
レコード	reko-do	record

レストラン	resutoran	restaurant
ワイシャツ	waishatsu	business shirt

Now you all are well aware of Katakana letters. But in Katakana, few exceptions are also there. Let us have a look at all those exceptions so that we will be able to read Katakana fluently without any hurdles. These exceptions are as follows –

1. We have learned in the modifiers rule of Hiragana that all i-ending consonants will get added with small ya, yu, and yo to get different phonetics. The same rule is applicable for Katakana.

2. Even though in Katakana we have the modifiers or the double consonant effect or contracted consonants, It is not sufficient to get a few foreign words to be transcribed into Japanese.

3. Katakana came up with a few additional sounds. They are as follows.

クヮ – kwa	クィ – kwi		クェ – kwe	クォ – kwo
			ギェ – gye	
グヮ – gwa	グィ – gwi		グェ – gwe	グォ – gwo
	スィ – Si			
			シェ – she	
	ズィ – zi			
			ジェ – je	

	ティ – ti			テュ – tyu
			チェ – che	
ツァ – tsa	ツィ – tsi		ツェ – tse	ツォ – tso
	ディ – di			デュ – dyu
			ニェ – nye	
		ホゥ – hu		
			ヒェ – hye	
ファ – fa	フィ – fi		フェ – fe	フォ – fo
フャ – fya	フュ – fyu	フョ – fyo		
			ビェ – bye	
			ピェ – pye	
			ミェ – mye	
			リェ – rye	
	ウィ – wi		ウェ – we	

These are a few of the exceptions we will get to find while reading statements or words with Katakana. Keen observation will help to read the statement properly. Let us learn a few grammar rules now. As now you will be able to read properly, understanding is the next part. Thus grammar will help us understand the meaning.

Chapter 6: Kanji

As discussed earlier, The Kanji is the pictorial presentation of an object. Hiragana indicates only the pronunciation of the word, but Kanji represents the exact meaning of the word. for e.g., はし

橋 – はし – bridge

箸 – はし – chopsticks

Both are pronounced as hashi, but both have different meanings. This is why we use Kanji while writing. Even though Kanji seems to be complicated, if learned with the basic details, i.e., with the help of radicals used in it, Kanji is one of the おもしろい or interesting parts.

The complicated Kanjis can be broken down into smaller components, and all those components are called characters. A few of the radicals can be a Kanji on their own. There are thousands of Kanjis in Japanese. A working adult in Japanese knows around 2700-3000 Kanjis. Let us begin the journey towards Kanjis. In this part of Kanjis, we will learn a few of the basic Kanjis. Keep practicing, and then things will surely be easy for you.

1. Every Kanji has got its own meaning.

2. But there are two types of pronunciations for every of the Kanji, namely onyomi or kunyomi.

3. おんよみ reading retains the original Chinese pronunciation, whileくんよみ reading is the revised reading using and mentioned with Japanese alphabets.

4. On reading is used when more than two Kanjis are paired together to form a word. Kun reading is used when Kanji stands alone or with Hiragana.

5. If you identified the radicals in the Kanjis, you would probably understand the meaning of the kanjis.

6. The easiest way to learn Kanjis is to learn the radicals.

Let us learn Kanjis of numbers from one to 10, and you will see that writing in Kanjis is way beyond easy if we understand it properly.

Numbers

Number	Hiragana	Pronunciation	Kanji	Meaning	On-reading	Kun-reading
1	いち	ichi	一	one	イチ イツ	ひと
2	に	ni	二	Two	ニ	ふた
3	さん	san	三	Three	サン	み みっ
4	よん or し	yon	四	Four	シ	よん よ よっ
5	ご	go	五	Five	ゴ	いつ
6	ろく	roku	六	six	ロク	むい む むっ

7	しち or なな	Shichi or nana	七	Seven	シチ	なな
						なの
8	はち	hachi	八	eight	ハチ	やつ
						よう
						や
9	きゅう	kyuu	九	Nine	キュウ	ここの
					ク	
10	じゅう	jyuu	十	Ten	ジュウ	とお
					ジュ	と

Hiragana   Kanji   pronunciation   Meaning

Hiragana	Kanji	pronunciation	Meaning
ついたち	一日	tsuitachi	first day of the month
ひとつ	一つ	hitotsu	one thing
ふつか	二日	futsuka	second day of the month
ふたつ	二つ	futatsu	two things
ふたり	二人	futari	two people
みっか	三日	mikka	third day of the month
みっつ	三つ	mittsu	three things
よっか	四日	yokka	fourth day of the month

よっつ	四つ	tottsu	four things
いつか	五日	itsuka	fifth day of the month
むいか	六日	muika	sixth day of the month
むっつ	六つ	muttsu	six things
なのか	七日	nanoka	seventh day of the month
ななつ	七つ	nanatsu	seven things
ようか	八日	youka	eighth day of the month
やっつ	八つ	yattsu	eight things
ここのか	九日	kokonoka	ninth day of the month
ここのつ	九つ	kokonotsu	nine things
とおか	十日	tooka	tenth day of the month
とお	十	too	ten things

This is the list of a few of the words using Kanjis which we learned earlier. Practice it. Understand a few of the Kanjis used in the above words.

日 ニチ ひ、び、か sun, day, counter for weekdays

人 ニン ジン ひと、り、と person

We know to write Kanjis of the first ten numbers and their pronunciation too. This is more than enough to understand how to write numbers till 99. Try it with your logic of understanding. Hint, eleven will be pronounced as **jyuuichi**, i.e., **じゅういち**, and in Kanji, it will be written as 十一. Likewise, give an attempt till 99 without looking at the table below.

11	じゅういち	十一		21	にじゅういち	二十一	
12	じゅうに	十二		22	にじゅうに	二十二	
13	じゅうさん	十三		23	にじゅうさん	二十三	
14	じゅうよん	十四		24	にじゅうよん	二十四	
15	じゅうご	十五		25	にじゅうご	二十五	
16	じゅうろく	十六		26	にじゅうろく	二十六	
17	じゅうしち	十七		27	にじゅうしち	二十七	
18	じゅうはち	十八		28	にじゅうはち	二十八	
19	じゅうきゅう	十九		29	にじゅうきゅう	二十九	
20	にじゅう	二十		30	さんじゅう	三十	

In the empty column beside, practice writing the numbers in Hiragana while reading out loud. You might have noticed that writing a number in Kanji is quite easy and short as compared to the word length of Hiragana. The only important thing is we must be aware of Kanjis of the numbers. You might have understood the concept of writing numbers. Now keep going and try writing all the numbers till 99. The multiples of 10 are as follows. Make your own chart of numbers.

60	ろくじゅう	六十	
70	しちじゅう	七十	
80	はちじゅう	八十	
90	きゅうじゅう	九十	
100	ひゃく	百	
1000	せん	千	
10000	まん	万	

There are a few exceptions while writing multiples of 100. Let us learn those exceptions.

100	ひゃく	百	
200	にひゃく	二百	
300	**さんびゃく**	三百	
400	よんひゃく	四百	
500	ごひゃく	五百	
600	**ろっぴゃく**	六百	
700	**ななひゃく**	七百	
800	**はっぴゃく**	八百	
900	きゅうひゃく	九百	

NOTE – See, the highlighted numbers in the above table are nothing but exceptions. While writing in Kanji, there is no need to put more effort, but while pronunciation or writing with Hiragana, you need to know this difference.

Clock –

If you people know numbers, then it is very easy to identify what the time is. In Japanese, a wall clock is called a とけい. Let us learn how to tell the time in Japanese.

Consider a situation if someone asks you,

いまなんじですか。

Ima nan ji desu ka.

Question – いまなんじですか。What is the time now?

Answer – いま**いちじ**です。It is one o'clock now.

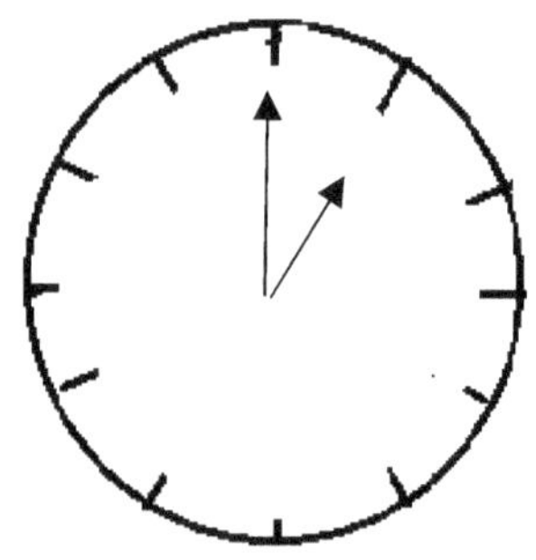

Question – いまなんじですか。What is the time now?

Answer – いま**にじ**です。 It is two o'clock now.

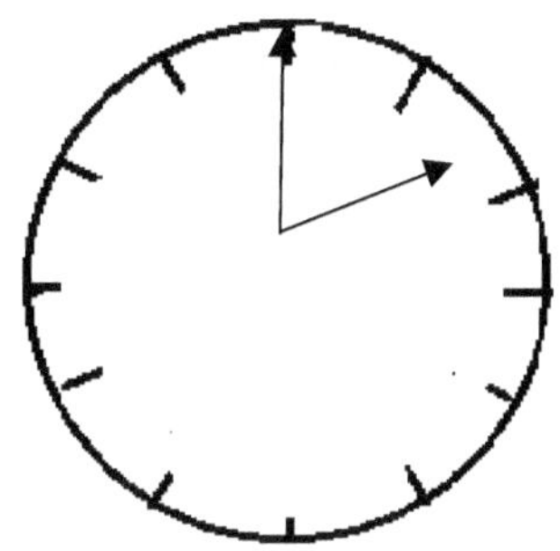

Likewise for the next hours follow the chart below

3 o'clock	さんじです。
4 o'clock	**よじです。**
5 o'clock	ごじです。
6 o'clock	ろくじです。
7 o'clock	しちじです。
8 o'clock	はちじです。
9 o'clock	**くじです。**
10 o'clock	じゅうじです。
11 o'clock	じゅういちです。
12 o'clock	じゅうにじです。

Weekdays-

For weekdays, counter ようび -- 曜日 is used. 曜 **this is an 18 stroke Kanji. We** don't need to discuss such a difficult Kanji at this level as a beginner. This Kanji means weekday, and as studied earlier, 日 represents a day. Go through the table below to know the names of all the days of the week.

Day	Hiragana	Kanji	Meaning of Kanji used.
Monday	げつようび	月曜日	月　moon, month
Tuesday	かようび	火曜日	火　fire
Wednesday	すいようび	水曜日	水　water
Thursday	もくようび	木曜日	木　tree, wood
Friday	きんようび 金曜日	金曜日	金　gold
Saturday	どようび	土曜日	土　soil, earth, ground
Sunday	にちようび	日曜日	日　sun, day

Month

Names of the month are easiest to remember. We just need to know the respective number and counter がつ 月 that is used to represent the name of a month. Let us go through the names of the month and let us understand corresponding Kanjis also.

Name of the month	Hiragana	Kanji
January	いちがつ	一月
February	にがつ	二月
March	さんがつ	三月
April	**しがつ**	**四月**
May	ごがつ	五月
June	ろくがつ	六月
July	しちがつ	七月
August	はちがつ	八月
September	**くがつ**	**九月**
October	じゅうがつ	十月
November	じゅういちがつ	十一月
December	じゅうにがつ	十二月

As you can see, writing in Kanjis is very easy. The only thing is you need to understand the meaning of Kanji and its pronunciation too.

Chapter 7: Grammar

Statement formation

In Japanese statements, formation is quite different from that of English. Let us compare both these so that it will be easy to mark the meaning of the statement.

English statement formation –

> Subject + Verb + Object

The subject of the statement is the person or place or the thing that is performing the action of the statement, i.e., verb.

The verb is the action word mentioned in the statement, which is to be performed by the subject of the statement.

The object can be defined as the person or thing who/which receives the action which is performed by the subject of the statement.

These meanings of the subject, object, or verb are going to be the same in Japanese statement formation. But the formation of a statement is quite different. It will be as follows,

> Subject + Object+ Verb

If you understood this concept, it wouldn't be much difficult to translate the statements from Japanese to English or vice versa.

E.g., In English,

I eat Mango.

--------→ (subject – I, verb – eat, object – Mango)

In Japanese, it will be,

わたしはマンゴーをたべます。

--------→ (subject - わたし- I, object - マンゴー - Mango, verb - たべます – eat. は and を are particles used in Japanese statement formation, which we will learn in-depth in subsequent topics.

In the following statements, you will find the same pattern.

あなたはコーヒーをのみますか。

Anata **wa** kohi **o** nomimasu ka?

Will you drink coffee?

そのいぬはミルクをのむ。

Sono inu wa miruku o nomu.

That dog drinks milk.

わたし**の**おとうと**は**あした**とうきょう**にいきます。

Watashi no otouto wa ashita toukyou ni ikimasu.

Tomorrow my younger brother will go to Tokyo.

ちち**は**よるごはん**の**あとでさんぽします。

Chichi wa yorugohan no ato de sanpo shimasu.

My father goes for a walk after dinner.

さんにん**の**こども**が**こうえんであそんでいます。

Sannin no kodomo ga kouen de asondeimasu.

Three children were playing in the park.

わたし**は**ここでおります。

Watashi wa koko de orimasu.

I will get off here/ I will get down here.

しじん**は**し**を**かく。

Shijin was hi o kaku.

The poet writes a poem.

わたし**は**そのほん**が**よみたい。

Watashi was ono hon ga yomitai.

I want to read that book.

かれはケーキをたべたい。

Kare wa ke-ki o tabetai.

I want to eat a cake.

かばんのいろはあかいです。

Kaban no iro wa akai desu.

The color of the bag is red.

You might have understood a little about how to break down the statement in order to understand it or to make meaning out of it. All the highlighted letters are particles, which is a very important topic from Japanese grammar. These particles will help us to understand the proper meaning of the statement. We will learn many points about particles in the next topic.

Chapter 8: Particles

Particles are small words that define the relationship between the words used in a statement. As a beginner, we need to know a few particles. The Japanese word for particles is じょし. Yes, you read it correctly, jyoshi(joshi). There are a total of 188 particles in Japanese. But the best part is, we don't need to learn them all. Basic 15 Japanese particles will be enough to understand the meaning of a statement. They are は, が, か, の, も, を, に, で, へ, と, や, から, まで, ね, and よ. See, it is like we are learning basic Japanese all over again. As we will go into this concept deeper, we will come to know that there is a lot more to explore about Japanese. Thus this is the most interesting language. Let us now explore and understand the use of very important and basic particles in the Japanese language.

は

When the letter は, works as a particle, it is pronounced as **wa**.

This particle is known as '**topic marker,**' as it mentions the main topic of the statement. This topic could be the subject, object, or verb. It completely depends on what the statement is about.

Generally, this particle wa comes after the subject of the statement.
Phrases while wishing good afternoon or good evening, i.e., konnichiwa, konbanwa, in both these cases wa is a topic marker, it is written as こんにちは、こんばんは respectively.
To mention the contract in two statements, particle wa is used.

This particle may follow a few other particles as well.

Examples will help to understand this properly.

わたしはマリアです。

 Watashi wa Maria desu.

I am Maria. --→ (です – is, am, are)

きょうはげつようびです。

 Kyou wa getsuyoubi desu.

 Today is Monday.

いぬはすきです。でも、うまはきらいです。

 Inu wa suku desu. Demo, uma wa kirai desu.

 I like horses. But I don't like dogs.

やまださんはにほんじんです。

 Yamada san wa nihonjin desu.

 Mr. Yamada is Japanese.

And likewise, we can use particle wa. I am sure you are getting it. It is very easy. Let us

learn the next particle, i.e., particle が.

が

Particle ga acts as a subject particle as well as an object particle for specific verbs.

In the case of the subject particle, it indicates existence. i.e., it comes with verbs あります

(arimasu- have) andいます (imasu – exist).

It is used as a subject marker in a statement when it is introduced for the first time in a conversation. To put focus on the subject.

It also works as an object marker in a few of the cases. In the case of statement patterns using ＿＿ほしいです and ＿たいです which indicates the desire, particle ga is used.

For e.g.

しつもんがあります。

Shitsumon ga arimasu.

I have a question.

NOTE – When no Subject is mentioned in a random statement, by default わたし- I is considered as a subject in those cases.

ペットがいます。

Petto ga imasu.

I have a pet.

じゅぎょうがありません。

Jyugyou ga arimasen.

I don't have class today.

わたしはじかん**が**ほしいです。

Watashi wa jikan **ga** hoshii desu.

I want time.

わたしはジュース**が**のみたいです。

Watashi wa jyu-su **ga** nomitai desu.

I want to drink Juice.

NOTE – In a few statements, が comes after the verb. There it acts as a conjunction and not as a particle.

の

Particle 'no' is the possessive particle. It is used to show that something belongs to someone or someone who possesses something.

It is used for both in the case of a noun as well as a pronoun.

It is also used to mention the category, origin, or material which belongs to someone. As mentioned in example no. 2 below.

To show that someone belongs to a university, particle の is used.

for e.g.

これはたなかさん**の**ほんです。

Kore wa tankasan no hon desu.

This is Tanakasan's book.

かれはにほんごのせんせいです。

Kare wa eigo no sensei desu.

He is the teacher of Japanese. -◊ Wordy meaning of the statement.

 He is a Japanese teacher. -◊Actual meaning of the statement.

しずかさん**の**かんがえはおもしろいです。

Shizukassan no kangae wa omoshiroi desu.

The idea of Miss. Shizuka is interesting. -◊ Wordy meaning of the statement.

Miss. Shizuka's idea is interesting. -◊ Actual meaning of the statement.

を

It is known as an object marker.

It comes after the direct object of an action mentioned in the verb of the statement.

It is also used to indicate the place of movement, i.e., with the verbs like

あるきます, とびます, わたります, まがります.

While requesting for something, particle を is used.

When it acts as an article, it is pronounced as **o**, i.e., equivalent to **お**.

for e.g.

わたしはケーキ**を**たべます。

Watashi wa ke-ki o tabemasu.

I eat cake.

わたしはあたらしいかばんをかいました。

Watashi wa atarashii kaban wo kaimashita.

I bought a new car.

みよこさんはすしをつくります。

Miyokosan wa sushi o tsukurimasu.

Miyoko makes sushi.

みずをください。

Mizu o kudasai.

Please give me water.

かのじょはこうさてんをわたります。

Kanono wa kousaten o watarimasu.

She crosses the intersection.

へ

When it acts as a particle in the statement, it is pronounced as **e.**

It is known as a direction particle or is used while indicating a goal.

for e.g.

わたしはインドへいきます。

Watashi wa Indo e ikimasu.

I go to India.

わたしはうちへかえります。

Watashi wa uchi e kaerimasu.

I returned home.

ともだちとこうえへいきます。

Tomodachi to kouen e ikimasu.

I am going to the park with my friends.

かれへメールをしました。

Kare e meru o shimashita.

I emailed him.

に

This article is used in a statement to indicate a location, time, time duration, date, or purpose.

While using it as a location marker, it denotes existence. i.e., with あります and います.

Also, to mention the workplace or the place where someone lives, i.e., with the verbs すみ

ます and つとめます, the particle に is used.

When it works as a time marker, it works as 'on,' 'in,' and 'at' in English.

This particle doesn't come with relative time expressions such as tomorrow, this month,

Last year, i.e., あした,こんげつ, きょねんlikewise words.

for e.g.

つくえのしたにいぬがいます。

Tsukue no shita ni inu ga imasu.

There is a dog under the table.

かれはIBMかいしゃにつとめます。

Kare wa IBM kaisha ni tsutomemasu.

He works for an IBM Company.

ろくじにやくそくがあります。

Roku ji ni yakusoku ga arimasu.

I have an appointment at six o'clock.

かようびにそうじをします。

Kayoubi ni souji o shimasu.

I clean on Tuesday.

で

This particle is used to mention a mode of transport or a means of doing something.

It is known as a location particle and sometimes as a means particle.

In the case of the location marker, it is used to show the place where the action mentioned in the verb took place.

Also used to indicate the material that is made up from something, i.e., it works as 'with,' 'from' or 'out of' in English.

It is used while highlighting the reason behind something.

for e.g.

だいがくでにほんごのべんきょうします。

Daigaku de Nihongo no benkyou shimasu.

I study Japanese at college.

きっさてんでコーヒーをかいました。

Kissaten de ko-hi- o kaimashita.

I bought coffee at the coffee shop.

わたしはバスでかいしゃにいきます。

Watashi wa basu de kaisha ni ikimasu.

I am going to the company by bus.

かのじょはほうちょうでやさいをきりました。

Kanojo wa houchou de yasai o kirimashita.

She cut the vegetables with a knife.

みよこさんはきでいすをつくりました。

Miyokosan wa ki de isu o tsukurimashita.

Miss. Miyoko made a chair out of wood.

と

This particle means 'and' in English. It can be referred to as coordinating conjunction, which is used to write two or more nouns.

To indicate the involvement, i.e., it is also used to mention 'with' or 'together.'

for e.g.

パンとさとうとたまごをください。

Pan to satou to tamago o kudasai.

Please give me bread, sugar, and egg.

ぎゅうにゅうとパンがすきです。

Gyuunyuu to pan ga suki desu.

I like milk and bread.

あしたしずかさんとデートをします。

Ashita Shizuka san to de-to o shimasu.

Tomorrow, I'll go on a date with Shizuka.

か

This is referred to as a question particle.

To frame a question, we need to add the particle 'ka' at the end of the statement. The formation of the statement becomes like this:

Subject + Object + Verb +か

It is also used to indicate alternatives or choices, i.e., it also works as 'or' in English.

For e.g.

たなかさんはアメリカじんです**か**。

Tanakasan wa Amerika jin desu ka.

Is Tanaka American?

たなかさんはえいごができます**か**。

Tanakasan wa eigo ga dekimasu ka.

Can Tanaka speak English?

にほんのりょうりはおいしいです**か**。

Nihon no ryouri wa oishii desu ka.

Is Italian food delicious?

くるま**か**バイクでとうきょうにいきたいです。

Kuruma ka baiku de toukyou ni ikitai desu.

I would like to go to Tokyo by car or bike.

も

This particle follows the noun.

In English, it means 'too' or 'also.'

It also emphasizes the amount or extent of something, i.e., in English, it acts as 'as many as' or 'as much as.'

for e.g.

ほんださんはにほんじんです。みよこさん**も**にほんじんです。

Hondasan wa nihonjin desu. Miyokosan mo nihonjin desu.

Honda is Japanese. Miss Miyoko is also Japanese.

わたし**も**です。

Watashi mo desu.

Me also/too.

これ**も**かわです。

Kore mo kawa desu.

This is also a river.

そのまんがはじゅっかい**も**よみました。

Sono manga wa jukkai mo yomimashita.

I read that manga as much as ten times.

スーパーで500ドル**も**つかいました。

Su-pa-de gohyaku doru mo tsukaimashita.

I spent as much as 500 dollars at the supermarket.

から

This is used to indicate from where or when (time) something starts.

In English, it means 'from,' i.e., it marks the starting point.

It always follows a noun i.e., _______から.

It is also used in the case to mention the material.

This is only used when the material doesn't appear in its original form.

for e.g.

ごじ**から**かいぎがあります。

Go ji kara kaigi ga arimasu.

There is a meeting from 3 o'clock.

とうきょう**から**おおさかはちかいです。

Toukyou kara oosaka wa chikai desu.

Osaka is near Tokyo.

こめ**から**おさけをつくります。

Kome kara osake wo tsukurimasu.

I make osake from rice.

まで

It means 'up to', 'to', or 'until' in English.

It marks the time or place when an action mentioned in the verb will end.

For e.g.

あさって**まで**まちます。

Asatte made machimasu.

I will wait until the day after tomorrow.

しけんは**ろくじまで**です。

Shiken wa roku ji made desu.

The exam is until six o'clock.

Chapter 9: Verbs & Adjectives

Verbs in Japanese are known as doushi, i.e., どうし. Verbs are classified into three types in Japanese. Namely, ichidan, godan, and the irregular verb. Let us understand a few of the basics one by one below.

いちだんどうし – ichidan-doushi -----→Group 2 verb

All the verbs ending with ru, when in their root form or dictionary form, are categorized under this type.

The starting part of the verb never changes, and it is called the **'stem part'** of a verb.

The part which changes according to the requirement of the type of verb needed in the statement is called **a suffix.**

We will be discussing five forms of these types of verbs in this topic, namely the root verb, ません-form, ます-form, and the volitional form.

This is called ichidandoushi, i.e., one step verb, because the stem part remains the same in the dictionary, masu, plain negative, imperative, and volitional form.

Let us look at the different forms of verb たべる,

Dictionary form たべる

ない-form たべない

ます-form たべます

Imperative form たべろ

Let's form たべよう

Basically, these verbs are used in two different ways — the first one in a casual way and the other one in a polite way. The polite version is often used while talking to everyone except friends or family. Thus ます-form indicates the polite way. Here onwards, we will stick to the ます-form.

Dictionary form	ます-form Present/Future	ます-form Past tense	Negative form	To ask question Do you?	Volitional (Let's)
たべる To eat	たべます	たべました	たべません	たべますか	たべましょう
みる To see	みます	みました	みません	みますか	みましょう
おきる To get up	おきます	おきました	おきません	おきます	おきましょう
ねる To lie down/ sleep	ねます	ねました	ねません	ねますか	ねましょう
きる To cut	きります	きりました	きりません	きりますか	きりましょう。

Let us understand the proper use of these verbs with a few conversations and a few easy statements.

Statements

くだものはきりましたか。

Kudamono wa kirimashita ka.

Did you cut the fruits?

ケーキをたべますか。

Ke-ki o tabemasu ka.

Will you eat cake/Do you eat cake?

テレビをみましょうか。

Terebi o mimashou ka.

Should we watch television together?

Conversation one

In the morning, two friends, A and B, are having a conversation at A's home.

A ： おはようございます。	Good morning.
あなたはあさごはんをたべましたか。	Did you eat breakfast?
B ：いいえ。	No.
たべていません。	I didn't eat yet.
いっしょにたべましょうか。	Should we eat together?
A ：はい。そうですか。	Yes. Is that so?
いっしょにたべましょう。	Let's eat together.

Conversation two

Two friends, Yuko and Satomi, are meeting at school after 2-3 days of the holidays and discussing in the classroom when one of them completed the homework.

ゆこ：	さとみさん、こんにちは。	Yuko: Hello Satomi.
	だいじょうぶですか。	Are you okay?
さとみ：はい。		Satomi: Yes.
	だいじょうぶです。	All good.
	きょう、なんじにおきましたか。	When did you wake up today?
ゆうこ：	ろくじにおきました。	Yuko: I woke up at 6.
さとみ：はい。そうですか。		Satomi: Yes. Is that so.
	なんじにねましたか。	At what time did you sleep?
ゆうこ：	きのう、じゅういちじにねました。	Yuko: Yesterday, I slept at 11.
さとみ：しゅくだいはいつしましたか。		Satomi: When did you complete the homework?
ゆうこ：しゅくだいはきのうはちじにしました。		Yuko: I completed the homework at 8 yesterday.
さとみ：すごいですね。		Satomi: Great.

ごだんどうし – godan-doushi ----➔ Group 1 verb

In this case, the dictionary form usually ends with a 'u' vowel.

If a verb is written in roman, the part of the verb except for the last letter u remains constant in every form and is known as the stem part of the verb.

In the chart below, the highlighted part is the stem part.

This is known as godandoushi, i.e., five steps verb, because it has a separate stem form each for dictionary, masu, plain negative, imperative, and volitional form.

Dictionary form	ます-form Present/Future	ます-form Past tense	Negative form	To ask question Do you?	Volitional form (Let's)
	Remove u+い series of corresponding letter +ます				
かく **kak**u To write	かきます	かきました	かきません	かきますか	かきましょう
たつ **tats**u To stand	たちます	たちました	たちません	たちますか	たちましょう
はなす **hanas**u To talk	はなします	はなしました	はなしません	はなしますか	はなしましょう
のむ **nom**u To drink	のみます	のみました	のみません	のみますか	のみましょう
きく **kik**u To listen	ききます	ききました	ききません	ききますか	ききましょう

There are many such verbs. Now you will be able to segregate between verbs ending with ru and verbs ending with u, both will have a different stem part, and thus ます-form of the respective words differ. Now let us understand the third and the last form of verbs, i.e., irregular verbs.

Statements

コーヒーはのみますか。

Kohi wa nomimasu ka.

Do you drink coffee?

こんどはいつあいましょうか。

Kondo wa itsu aimashou ka.

When shall we meet next?

またあさってあいましょう。

Mata asatte aimashou.

Let's meet again the day after tomorrow.

Irregular

This consists of only two verbs.

Both these verbs are irregular thus need to be memorised.

Here we will discuss the dictionary, masu, plain negative, imperative and volitional form.

The two verbs are   する – to do

　　　　　　　くる – to come

Dictionary form	Plain negative	ます-form	Imperative	Volitional
する	しない	します	しろ	しよう
くる	こない	きます	こい	こよう

We have already discussed a few of the statements, including します and きます.

In this way, we have completed all these three types of verbs. Let us now perform an activity. A few of the verbs and their meanings are mentioned below. You have to identify the type of verb.

Verb Meaning いちだんどうし ごだんどうし

つける to turn on

つく to arrive

やすむ to take a day off

いく to go

あるく to walk

しめる to close

つとめる to work for

よむ to read

できる to be able to

すう to smoke

みせる to show

つかう to use

おす to push

Mark the corresponding verb, if it is **ichidandoushi** or **godandoushi**. Remember, endings with ru are nothing but ichidan-doushi, and endings with u are godan-doushi.

<u>Adjective</u>

Adjectives in Japanese areけいようし. There are two types of adjectives in Japanese, namely

い-adjectives and な-adjectives.

い - adjectives – All the adjectives ending with い are known as い-adjectives or いけいようし.

for e.g., かわいい

おおきい

な-adjectives – The adjectives which don't end with い are known as な-adjectives or なけい

ようし. But there are also a few exceptions. Thus, we need to memorize all these adjectives.

for e.g., すき

きれい

ひま

Depending on the type of adjective and if we want to use this adjective in an assertive or negative form, there are certain rules for this.

<u>い - adjectives</u>

Negative

To make i-adjective sound negative, remove い and add くない.

for e.g., おおきい ———>おおきくない

Past

To make past tense, remove い and add かった.

for e.g., おおきい ———>**おおきかった**

Past Negative

To make the past tense negative, remove い and add くなかった.

for e.g. おおきい ———>**おおきくなかった**

<u>な -adjectives</u>

Negative

To make な-adjective negative, add じゃない.

for e.g. すき----->すきじゃない

Past

To make past, add でした.

For e.g., すき----->すきでした

Past Negative

To make the past tense negative, remove い and add かった.

for e.g. すき----->すきじゃない ———>すきじゃなかった

Let us learn a few more **い-adjectives and な-adjectives.**

い- adjectives	Meaning	な- adjectives	Meaning
おおきい	Big	すてき	Lovely
ちいさい	Small	ゆうめい	Famous
ながい	Long	しずか	Silent
みじかい	Short	にぎやか	Lively
あつい	Hot	げんき	Healthy
つめたい	Cold	びょうき	Ill
やすい	Inexpensive	しんせつ	Kind
たかい	Costly	すき	Like

To learn how to use these adjectives, observe the following pictures and statements below them.

たかい くるま

あつい コーヒー

やすい やさい

しろい たまご

ながいえんぴつとしろいかみです。

We have learned many things about Japanese. There is still a lot more to learn. You keep practicing. Japanese is a very vast but interesting language. The more we study, the more we will get to know about it. See you in the next part of this book. There we will read a few of the stories with a breakdown of statements.

My final request…

Being a smaller author, reviews help me tremendously!

It would mean the world to me if you could leave a review.

If you liked reading this book and learned a thing or two, please let me know!

It only takes 30 seconds but means so much to me!

Thank you and I can't wait to see your thought.

Conclusion

I know that this journey from a complete beginner in the Japanese language to having sufficient knowledge about Japanese scripts, their cultural expressions, and a few of the topics from the grammar section has been interesting. There is a song named 'Make me a child again' sung by artist Frankie laine. If you have never listened to this song, take a moment and listen to it. I'm not aware of if we will get a second birth or if we get to experience childhood again, but while learning a new language, we truly get to experience this being a child thing. We get an opportunity to rediscover the old us. De facto, Japanese is one of the picture-oriented languages, where we get a chance to think to implement our own ideas, and it awakens the kind of curiosity which keeps on growing. Also, this language is so vast that you will never have a shortage of tasks to study. There are multiple animes, mangas, technologies. In fact, much more is there to discover about Japan. Thus learning Japanese is a never-ending process. With this book, you have got sufficient knowledge of Japanese rituals, scripts, and grammar. In my 2nd book, we will learn the implementation of all these points which we have learned in this book.

www.ingramcontent.com/pod-product-compliance
Lightning Source LLC
LaVergne TN
LVHW060345200726
843507LV00005B/973